18-

America's First Peoples

the Ojibwa

Wild Rice Gatherers

by Therese DeAngelis

Consultant:
Vikki Howard
Community Relations Coordinator
Department of American Indian Studies
University of Minnesota, College of Liberal Arts

Blue Earth Books
an imprint of Capstone Press
Mankato, Minnesota

Blue Earth Books are published by Capstone Press
151 Good Counsel Drive, P.O. Box 669, Mankato, Minnesota 56002
http://www.capstone-press.com

Copyright © 2003 by Capstone Press. All rights reserved.

No part of this book may be reproduced in whole or in part, or stored in a retrieval system, or transmitted in any form or by any means, electronic, mechanical, photocopying, recording, or otherwise, without written permission from the publisher. For information regarding permission, write to Capstone Press, 151 Good Counsel Drive, P.O. Box 669, Dept. R, Mankato, Minnesota 56002.
Printed in the United States of America

Library of Congress Cataloging-in-Publication Data
DeAngelis, Therese.
  The Ojibwa : wild rice gatherers / by Therese DeAngelis.
  p. cm. — (America's first peoples)
  Summary: Discusses the Ojibwa Indians, focusing on their tradition of gathering wild rice. Includes a rice recipe and instructions for making a dream catcher.
  Includes bibliographical references and index.
  ISBN-13: 978-0-7368-1537-6 (hardcover)   ISBN-10: 0-7368-1537-6 (hardcover)
  1. Ojibwa Indians—Juvenile literature. 2. Wild rice—Juvenile literature. [1. Ojibwa Indians. 2. Indians of North America. 3. Wild rice.] I. Title. II. Series.
E99.C6 D33 2003
977'.004973—dc21   2002012535

Editorial credits
Editor: Megan Schoeneberger
Series designer: Kia Adams
Photo researcher: Jo Miller
Product planning editor: Karen Risch

Cover images: women gathering wild rice from The American Aboriginal Portfolio by Seth and Mary Eastman, Stock Montage, Inc.; birchbark basket, North Wind Picture Archives

Photo credits
Ann and Rob Simpson, 6–7
Capstone Press/Gary Sundermeyer, 3 (both), 10 (left), 11, 24, 25 (all)
Corbis, 16–17, 20
Doranne Jacobson, 27 (right), 28 (left), 28–29
Marilyn "Angel" Wynn, 4–5, 8 (top left and bottom left), 12–13, 18, 21 (bottom)
Minnesota Historical Society, 12 (left), 22–23, 23 (right); Monroe P. Killy, 17 (right)
National Gallery of Art, Washington, Buffalo Chase in the Snow - Ojibwa, by George Catlin, 10 (right)
North Wind Picture Archives, 7 (right), 8–9
PhotoDisc, Inc., 29 (right)
Photri-Microstock, 14 (left), 19, 21 (top)
Ralph LaPlant, 26–27
Stock Montage, Inc., 14–15

1 2 3 4 5 6 08 07 06 05 04 03

Contents

Chapter 1	A New Home	4
Chapter 2	A Wild Rice Legend	6
Chapter 3	The Month of Making Rice	8
Chapter 4	Wild Rice Harvesting	12
Chapter 5	Drying the Rice	16
Chapter 6	Removing Chaff	18
Chapter 7	A First Rice Feast	22
Chapter 8	The Ojibwa Today	26

Features

Words to Know	30
To Learn More	30
Places to Write and Visit	31
Internet Sites	31
Index	32

Try a recipe for a wild rice breakfast on page 11.

Turn to page 21 to learn the Moccasin Game.

Make your own dream catcher on page 24.

Chapter One

A New Home

The Ojibwa people once lived along the Atlantic Coast of North America. They used small white shells called megis shells for trade and to keep track of agreements between tribes. The megis shell was very important to the Ojibwa. The people left their homeland to search for the Sacred Megis Shell.

Their search led them to a new home near the Great Lakes. The Ojibwa found tall wild rice plants floating on the lake water. They called their new home the place where "food grows on water."

The Ojibwa set up villages near the Great Lakes, where they found wild rice growing on the water.

The Ojibwa Name

The Ojibwa also are called the Chippewa. "Chippewa" is the French way of saying "Ojibwa." Many historians believe the Ojibwa name comes from the style of shoes the Ojibwa once wore. The stitches on their moccasins appeared wrinkled or folded. Other people called them "otchipwa," which means "puckered up moccasin." Other spellings of the nation's name include "Ojibwe," "Ojibway," and "Chippeway."

The Ojibwa call themselves "Anishinabe," which means "the first people." The Ottawa and Potawatomi tribes once called themselves Anishinabe as well. The Ojibwa, Ottawa, and Potawatomi were once a single group. They were called the Three Fires.

Chapter Two

A Wild Rice Legend

The Ojibwa believe that wild rice is a gift from Gitchi Manido, the Creator. Storytellers explain how the Ojibwa discovered wild rice.

One evening, a half-man, half-spirit named Nanaboozhoo (na-na-BOO-jou) had no meat to cook. Suddenly, he saw a duck fly away from the the edge of his cooking pot. When Nanaboozhoo looked into the pot, he saw strange grains floating in the hot water.

Nanaboozhoo was hungry. He swallowed the grains and water in the pot. It tasted like delicious soup. When the pot was empty, Nanaboozhoo followed the duck to the lake. He found many birds eating the same grains he had seen in his pot. After that day, Nanaboozhoo knew he could find food growing on the lake.

The Ojibwa believe a half-man, half-spirit named Nanaboozhoo discovered wild rice.

Wild rice is a grain that can be cooked and eaten.

Chapter Three

The Month of Making Rice

Each season offered different foods to the Ojibwa people. Beginning in mid-August, they harvested rice that had grown tall in the warm summer weather. They called this time "the month of making wild rice." In other seasons, the Ojibwa moved their camps to be closer to other sources of food.

In spring, the Ojibwa collected sap in birchbark buckets. Women then boiled the sap in large deerskin containers. As it warmed, the sap became thick syrup. Next, they poured the syrup into tubs. With wooden paddles, they cooked and stirred the syrup until it turned to sugar.

The Ojibwa used baskets and bowls to gather maple syrup.

The Ojibwa and other American Indians worked together to gather wild rice and other food.

In summer, the Ojibwa planted corn, squash, and pumpkins. They gathered raspberries, wild strawberries, wild plums, blackberries, and blueberries. They dried and stored the food for the cold winter.

In winter, Ojibwa hunters went into the forests near the Great Lakes. They trapped rabbit, fox, and beaver. They hunted ducks, geese, and other animals. To catch fish, they cut holes into the thick ice on lakes.

Wild rice did not grow in winter. During this time, the Ojibwa hunted for other food.

Make a Wild Rice Breakfast

Wild rice is a grain that gives energy. Mixed with berries and sweetened with syrup, it makes a tasty breakfast cereal.

What You Need

Ingredients

1 cup (240 mL) cooked wild rice, chilled
2 tablespoons (30 mL) raisins, blueberries, raspberries, or cranberries
2 teaspoons (10 mL) maple syrup
¼ cup (60 mL) milk

Equipment

small bowl
dry-ingredient measuring cups
measuring spoons
liquid measuring cup
small spoon

What You Do

1. Place wild rice in small bowl.
2. Add berries or raisins to wild rice.
3. Add maple syrup and milk. Mix together with a small spoon.

Makes 1 serving

Chapter Four

Wild Rice Harvesting

Each fall, small groups of Ojibwa traveled to find wild rice. A man and woman canoed through the rivers and lakes. Steering with a wooden pole, the man guided the birchbark canoe through the thick rice plants. The woman reached from the canoe, grabbing wild rice plants. She gently brushed the heads of the plants with two long paddles called knockers. The ripe grains fell into the canoe. When rice filled the canoe, the man and woman headed for shore.

The Ojibwa brushed wild rice from the plants with long, wooden sticks.

The Ojibwa used canoes for travel as well as for harvesting wild rice.

> The Ojibwa went to the same rice field many times to harvest the rice.

Rice gatherers worked slowly. Harvesting took several weeks. The gatherers sometimes went back to the same rice fields five or six times each season. Each time, they gathered more of the ripened rice, being careful to take only as much as they needed. They always left some grains so that the plants could grow again next season. They also left some rice for wild birds to eat.

The Ojibwa used sticks to brush the rice grains from the plant.

Chapter Five

Drying the Rice

The Ojibwa carefully prepared the rice harvest. They spread the rice on flat rocks or sheets of birchbark. In the warm sun, the rice dried slowly and turned brown.

After wild rice dries, it still is not ready to eat. The Ojibwa needed to loosen the outer shells of the rice. Women and girls parched the rice by pouring the rice into large tubs. Without adding water, they set the tubs over a fire. They stirred the rice constantly with large, flat paddles so the rice would not burn.

Parching wild rice over a fire loosened the outer shells of the rice.

The Ojibwa dried freshly harvested rice in the warm sun.

Chapter Six

Removing Chaff

The next step in rice harvesting was to separate the waste, called chaff, from the rice grains. The Ojibwa placed the parched rice in a large basket with slanted sides. Three or four people pounded the rice with long poles. They lifted the poles high and then dropped them along the sides of the basket. They had to be careful to shake off only the outer shells without breaking the rice grains. This process was called milling.

They then emptied the milled rice onto broad, flat birchbark trays. Women tossed the rice lightly into the air. Most of the chaff blew away, and the rice grain landed in the trays. This step was called winnowing.

Women tossed the rice gently into the air to remove the rice shells from the rice grain.

The Ojibwa sometimes used their hands to remove extra chaff after jigging.

To separate the last bit of chaff from the grain, harvesters placed the rice in a partly buried barrel called a "makakosag" (ma-KACK-o-sag). An Ojibwa man or young boy wearing clean, new deerskin boots climbed into the barrel. Gripping thick branches to hold himself up, he began to dance. He danced quickly and lightly, being careful not to break the grains. This jigging method separated the remaining chaff from the rice grains.

Moccasin Game

After a day of harvesting and preparing wild rice, Ojibwa people sometimes played games. In the moccasin game, a player would line up four moccasins and hide a stone or bead under one of them. The other players had to guess where the item was hiding. You can play a version of this game.

What You Need

four shoes
one marble
two or more players

What You Do

1. One player places the shoes in a line.
2. The other players close their eyes. The first player hides a marble under one of the shoes.
3. The other players take turns guessing where the marble is hidden. They lift a shoe to see if the marble is there. If they are correct, they get a point. If they are wrong, the next person can guess.

Chapter Seven

A First Rice Feast

After the rice was prepared, Ojibwa women cooked a First Rice feast to celebrate the harvest. They roasted wild birds and fish. They served the meat with fresh and dried berries. They boiled the rice with meat. They also cooked some of the rice in a bit of animal fat, which made it break open like popcorn.

Before the Ojibwa ate their meal, they honored Gitchi Manido. They placed dishes of food in the rice fields, in the woods where they camped, and along the water's edge. This food was their offering to Gitchi Manido. Even today, the Ojibwa remember to place a plate of rice outdoors for First Rice. They believe that Gitchi Manido's spirit lives in the animals that eat the rice.

The Ojibwa filled baskets like this one with wild rice and gave them as gifts to neighbors and visitors.

The Ojibwa cooked a feast to celebrate the first rice of the season.

Make a Dream Catcher

Ojibwa mothers, sisters, and grandmothers made dream catchers for new babies. The Ojibwa believed that dream catchers hanging over sleeping children trapped bad dreams. They believed good dreams passed through the open spaces in the web and slid down the feathers onto the sleeper.

Dream catchers can be made in many ways, but some parts are always the same. Dream catchers are made with eight points around a circle to stand for Spider Woman's eight legs. Ojibwa stories say Spider Woman was a tiny female spider who helped bring sun to the earth each morning. Traditional dream catchers include a feather inside the webbing. The feather stands for breath, or air. Beads were not used in original dream catchers. Today, people sometimes add beads to their dream catchers for decoration.

What You Need

paper plate
scissors
paper punch
yarn
blunt yarn needle
a few feathers
a few pony beads

What You Do

1. Cut out the center of the paper plate.
2. Punch eight holes around the edge of the paper plate.
3. Cut four lengths of yarn about 24 inches (61 centimeters) and tie one each to four of the holes on the edge of the plate.
4. Thread the blunt yarn needle with an end of one yarn piece. Weave the yarn through one of the open holes on the plate. Choose one hole to be the bottom and thread the last part of the yarn through this hole.
5. Repeat step 4 until all yarn pieces have been woven through the bottom hole. You may thread a pony bead through several of the yarn pieces before weaving them, if desired.
6. Tie the yarn pieces into a large knot at the bottom of the dream catcher.
7. Tie some pony beads or stick feathers onto the loose yarn ends, if desired.
8. Use another piece of yarn to make a hanging loop at the top of the dream catcher.
9. Hang the dream catcher near your bed.

Chapter Eight

The Ojibwa Today

Today, the Ojibwa live on more than 100 reservations and in communities in Michigan, Minnesota, Montana, North Dakota, and Wisconsin. The Ojibwa Nation in the United States has more than 100,000 members. An additional 76,000 Ojibwa live in Canada. They live in Ontario, Manitoba, and Saskatchewan. On reservations, the Ojibwa have their own businesses. They have stores, factories, and schools. Many Ojibwa work for the tribal government.

Ojibwa still harvest wild rice and make maple sugar. They live a modern way of life, but they also try to follow the customs of their ancestors. They feel strongly about preserving their culture and language. Men and women

Today, many Ojibwa still harvest wild rice.

Ojibwa children learn about and practice the traditions of their ancestors.

teach quillwork, beadwork, and birchbark crafts. They share their traditional dances and songs with others during seasonal celebrations.

The Ojibwa believe that it is important to pass on their traditional way of life. Their children learn about the customs that make them unique. The Ojibwa want all North Americans to understand the beautiful traditions of their tribe.

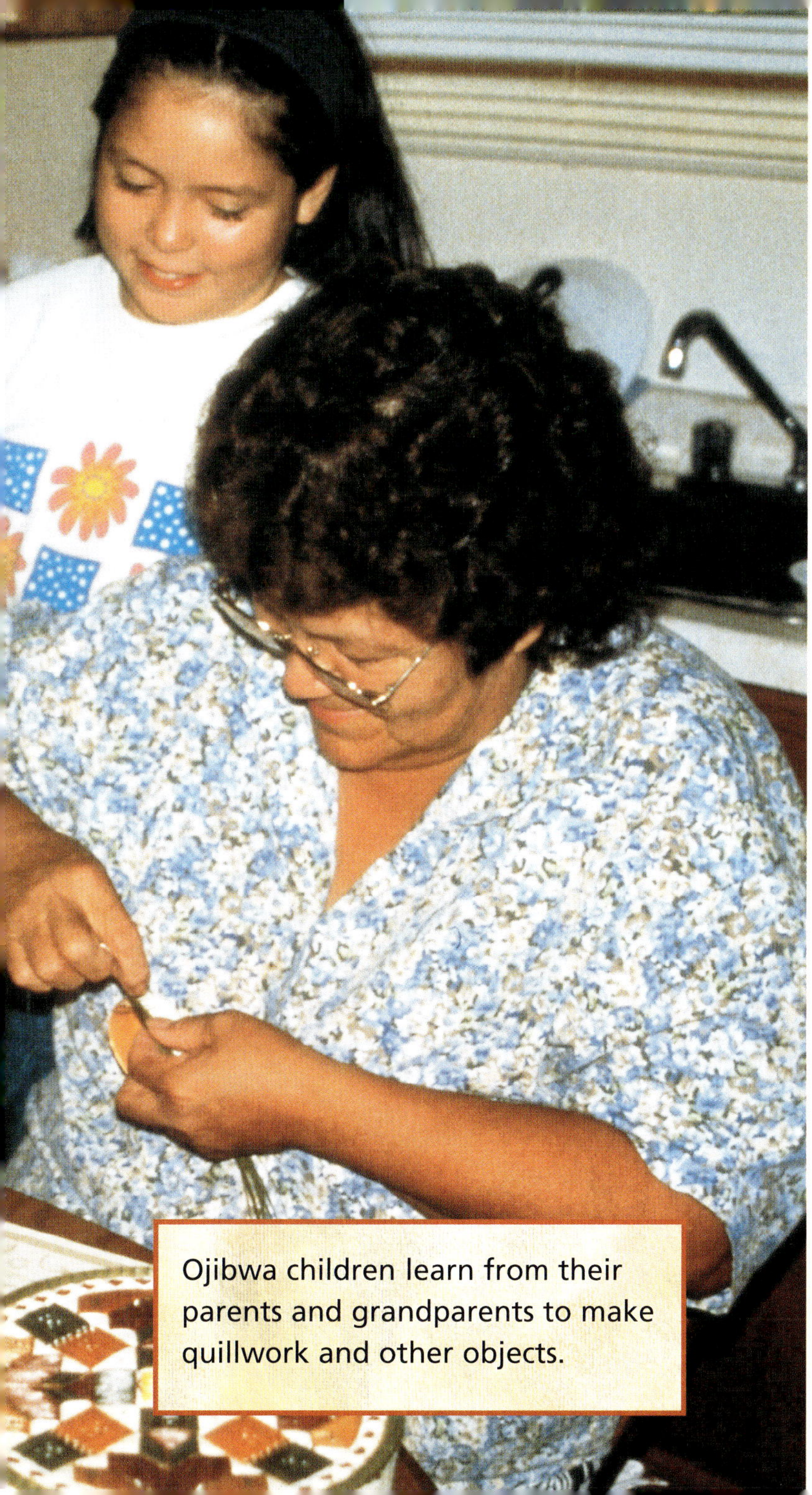

Ojibwa children learn from their parents and grandparents to make quillwork and other objects.

The Language of the Ojibwa

The Ojibwa language is called "Ojibwemowin." It is very descriptive. The word for chipmunk actually means "an animal that has spots between the stripes." The word for garage means "building where the car is kept."

Originally, Ojibwemowin was not a written language. Some Ojibwa have adapted letters from the English alphabet to put the language on paper. The Ojibwa language is changing with history. Even though computers or cars did not exist many years ago, the language now has words for them.

Words to Know

ancestor (AN-sess-tur)—a family member who lived a long time ago

chaff (CHAF)—the waste, such as grain coverings, that is separated from the seed when winnowing grain

harvest (HAR-vist)—to collect or gather crops that are ripe; the food that is gathered sometimes is called the harvest.

historian (hiss-TOR-ee-uhn)—a person who studies past events

parch (PARCH)—to make very dry

pucker (PUHK-ur)—to wrinkle or fold

reservation (rez-ur-VAY-shuhn)—land that the U.S. government sets aside for an American Indian nation to use

sacred (SAY-krid)—having to do with religion

syrup (SIHR-uhp)—a sweet, thick liquid

winnow (WIN-oh)—to remove waste by tossing lightly into the air

To Learn More

Erdrich, Louise. *The Birchbark House.* Thorndike, Maine: Thorndike Press, 2000.

Lund, Bill. *The Ojibwa Indians.* Native Peoples. Mankato, Minn.: Bridgestone Books, 1997.

Regguinti, Gordon. *The Sacred Harvest: Ojibway Wild Rice Gathering.* We Are Still Here. Minneapolis: Lerner Publications, 1992.

Todd, Anne M. *Ojibwa: People of the Great Lakes.* American Indian Nations. Mankato, Minn.: Bridgestone Books, 2003.

Places to Write and Visit

Bad River Band of Lake Superior Chippewa
Route 2
P.O. Box 39
Odanah, WI 54861

Lac Courte Oreilles Band of Lake Superior Chippewa
Route 2
Box 2700
Hayward, WI 54843

Museum of Ojibwa Culture
500-566 North State
St. Ignace, MI 49781

Sokaogon Mole Lake Chippewa Community
Route 1
Box 625
Crandon, WI 54520

Internet Sites

Track down many sites about the Ojibwa.
Visit the FACT HOUND at *http://www.facthound.com*

IT IS EASY! IT IS FUN!

1) Go to *http://www.facthound.com*
2) Type in: 0736815376
3) Click on "FETCH IT" and FACT HOUND will find several links hand-picked by our editors.

Relax and let our pal FACT HOUND do the research for you!

Index

basket, 8, 18, 23
beadwork, 28
berries, 10, 11, 22
birchbark, 8, 12, 16, 18, 28

canoe, 12, 13
chaff, 18, 20
children, 24, 27, 28, 29
corn, 10
Creator. See Gitchi Manido

dream catchers, 24–25

fall, 12
feast, 22, 23
First Rice, 22
fishing, 10

game, 21
Gitchi Manido, 6, 22

grain, 6, 7, 11, 12, 14, 15, 18, 19, 20
Great Lakes, 4, 5, 10

home, 4
hunting, 10

jigging, 20

knockers, 12

language, 26, 29

makakosag, 20
megis shell, 4
milling, 18
moccasin, 5, 21

name, 5
Nanaboozhoo, 6, 7

parching, 16

quillwork, 28, 29

reservation, 26

sap, 8
spring, 8
sugar, 8, 26
summer, 8, 10
syrup, 8, 11

Three Fires, 5
trade, 4

villages, 5

winnowing, 18, 19
winter, 10